SAN FRANCISCO BAY

by M. Weber

CHERRY LAKE PUBLISHING • ANN ARBOR, MICHIGAN

Published in the United States of America by:

CHERRY LAKE PRESS

2395 South Huron Parkway, Suite 200, Ann Arbor, MI 48104

www.cherrylakepublishing.com

Reading Adviser: Marla Conn MS, Ed., Literacy specialist, Read-Ability, Inc.

Series Adviser: Amy Reese, Coordinator of Elementary Science; Howard County School System, MD; President of Maryland Science Supervisors Association

Book Design: Book Buddy Media

Photo Credits: ©Mai Vu/Getty Images, background (pattern), ©Aziz Ary Neto/Getty Images, cover (front top), ©sevendeman/Getty Images, cover (bottom left), ©tamara_kulikova/Getty Images, cover (bottom right), ©iStockphoto/ Getty Images, cover (lined paper), ©Rainer Lesniewski/Getty Images, cover (map), ©Pixabay, cover (red circle), ©Devanath/Pixabay, (paperclips), ©louanapires/Pixabay, (paper texture), ©bluejayphoto/Getty Images, 1, ©GlobalP/ Getty Images, 3 (bottom left), ©tamara_kulikova/Getty Images, 3 (bottom right), ©MariuszBlach/Getty Images, 4, ©Hey Darlin/Getty Images, 6, ©polybutmono/Getty Images, 7, ©Crystal Eye Studio/Shutterstock, 8, ©WorldIslandInfo. com/Wikimedia, 9, ©Frank Chen Photography/Shutterstock, 10, ©Gregory Adams/Getty Images, 11, ©cbdgphoto/ Getty Images, 12, ©Glenn Price/Shutterstock, 13, ©Evan Linnell/Getty Images, 14, ©Diy13/Getty Images, 15 (top), ©Mint Images/Getty Images, 15 (bottom), ©divedog/Shutterstock, 16, ©eurotravel/Getty Images, 17, ©DavidCallan/ Getty Images, 18, ©MikeLane45/Getty Images, 19, ©Bkamprath/Getty Images, 20, ©pressdigital/Getty Images, 21 (top), ©jacktheflipper/Getty Images, 21 (bottom), ©Michael Urmann/Shutterstock, 22, ©Wilhelm Gottlieb Tilesius von Tilenau/Wikimedia, 23, ©Hero Images/Getty Images, 24, ©melhijad/Shutterstock, 25, ©Mark Wilson/ Staff/Getty Images, 26, ©SolStock/Getty Images, 27, ©matty2x4/Getty Images, 28 (scissors), ©Ilya_Starikov/ Getty Images, 28 (colored pencils), ©Muralinath/Getty Images, 29, ©Billy Huynh/Getty Images, cover (back)

Library of Congress Cataloging-in-Publication Data has been filed and is available at catalog.loc.gov

Cherry Lake Publishing would like to acknowledge the work of the Partnership for 21st Century Learning, a Network of Battelle for Kids. Please visit *http://www.battelleforkids.org/networks/p21* for more information.

Printed in the United States of America
Corporate Graphics

CONTENTS

CHAPTER 1
Introduction to San Francisco Bay 4

CHAPTER 2
The San Francisco Bay Watershed.............8

CHAPTER 3
Plants and Animals of
San Francisco Bay 12

CHAPTER 4
Impact on Plants and Animals 18

CHAPTER 5
Humans and the Bay..................................22

Activity...28
Glossary 30
For More Information 31
Index 32

CHAPTER 1

Introduction to San Francisco Bay

San Francisco Bay is located in Northern California. It is home to the Golden Gate Bridge. It is one of the most well-known bays in the country. It is 60 miles (97 kilometers) long and between 3 and 12 miles (5 to 19 km) wide. In addition to the Golden Gate Bridge, there are four other bridges that connect all sides of the bay.

San Francisco Bay was first visited by European settlers in 1769. Since then it has become an important port for shipping and transportation. Today the bay touches three important cities: San Francisco, San Jose, and Oakland. It is enjoyed by about 7 million people who live in the Bay Area. Many people visit the bay by boat. They travel on sailboats, yachts, and ferries.

All of the water in the bay is part of the Earth system known as the **hydrosphere**. San Francisco Bay is an **estuary**. An estuary is the place where a river meets another body of water. In the bay, freshwater from the Sacramento and San Joaquin Rivers meets saltwater from the Pacific Ocean. The water in the bay ranges from 53 degrees Fahrenheit (12 degrees Celsius) to 60°F (16°C).

* Golden Gate Bridge connects the city of San Francisco to Marin County.

Over 1,000 different types of animals live in the bay. The animals and plants are part of the **biosphere**. The estuary is especially important for fish and birds who thrive in both saltwater and freshwater **habitats**. The different habitats attract all types of wildlife. These include animals that are found nowhere else in the world. The bay is also a popular place for people to look for seals.

The San Andreas and Hayward fault lines run below the watershed of the bay. Fault lines exist beneath the ground. Over time, the movement of **tectonic plates** helps to shape the land above. The movement started around 560,000 years ago. This is how the boundaries of San Francisco Bay were created. This part of the bay belongs to the **geosphere** portion of the Earth's systems.

* Driving cars is one way people create pollution.

The cities near San Francisco Bay have impacted the **atmosphere** of the bay. The atmosphere is made up of air. Human activity creates **pollution** in the air. The increase in carbon dioxide can affect the ability of plants and animals to grow. Normally the air in the bay averages about 57°F (14°C), with an average rainfall of 23 inches (58 centimeters).

Together, the Earth's systems create a natural wonder in San Francisco Bay. It is the largest bay on the West Coast of the United States. It is an important home for animals, plants, and people.

CHAPTER 2

The San Francisco Bay Watershed

The Sacramento and San Joaquin Rivers flow southward toward the Pacific Ocean. They meet in San Francisco Bay. The Sacramento River is the largest river in California. It runs for about 400 miles (644 km). Its starting point is in the Klamath Mountains. The San Joaquin River is 366 miles (589 km) long. It begins in the Sierra Nevada Mountains. The two rivers join in the Sacramento–San Joaquin River **Delta** and flow into San Francisco Bay.

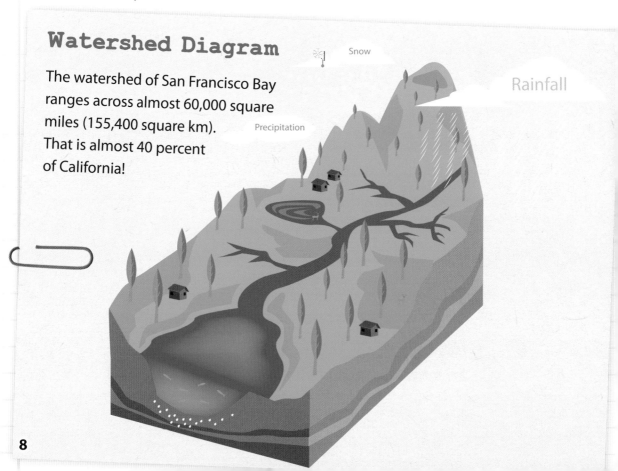

Watershed Diagram

The watershed of San Francisco Bay ranges across almost 60,000 square miles (155,400 square km). That is almost 40 percent of California!

Snow

Rainfall

Precipitation

The Sacramento–San Joaquin watershed supports farmland and crops.

The watershed is **vital** to the people of California. A watershed is an area of connected rivers, lakes, and bays. The Sacramento–San Joaquin River Delta is an area that is rich in farmland. It is also a source of freshwater for the state of California. The watershed provides much of the water that is used in cities and farmland in the state.

Between the delta and the ocean, there are three main bays that make up the San Francisco Bay estuary. These are Suisun Bay, San Pablo Bay, and San Francisco Bay. Most of the bay is very shallow. On average, it is only 15 to 17 feet (4.6 to 5.2 meters) deep. In some places, it is barely 1 foot (0.3 m) deep.

The estuary is the area where the freshwater from the rivers meets the Pacific Ocean. In the San Francisco Bay estuary, the water is **brackish**. Brackish water is a mix of saltwater and freshwater. This creates a brackish tidal marsh. A tidal marsh is created by water that flows into it from the river and ocean. It is also affected by the **tides** of the ocean.

* The plants that grow in the marshlands near San Francisco Bay need a mix of saltwater and freshwater to grow.

There are many types of tidal marshes. They are found in different areas of the bay. A tidal salt marsh has more saltwater than brackish water. Plants that can survive in the tidal salt marsh must be able to remove salt from the water in order to grow.

San Francisco Bay is known for its importance to California and the United States. In 2013, it was named a **Wetland** of International Importance by the U.S. government. The bay impacts many parts of California. It is important for both animals and people.

＊ During low tide, the soil in salt marshes drains slightly, allowing the plants that grow there enough air to maintain their roots.

CHAPTER 3

Plants and Animals of San Francisco Bay

There is an **abundance** of plant and animal life in San Francisco Bay. The bay covers a large area. All of the wildlife is connected through the watershed environments in the area. There is always life to be spotted in the rivers, marshes, or ocean waters. Birds, fish, and mammals live in the bay.

Many birds eat fish from the waters of San Francisco Bay.

San Francisco Bay is part of the Western Hemisphere Shorebird Reserve Network. A shorebird is any bird that lives near a shoreline. One example is Ridgway's rail. Ridgway's rail is a bird that lives in the salt marshes of San Francisco Bay. It **forages** near brackish water. Ridgway's rail is also one of the many endangered species living in the bay. Endangered animals are species with low populations. These species are at risk of disappearing.

The waters of San Francisco Bay are home to many different types of fish. The most well known are certain kinds of anchovies and salmon. The northern anchovy is one of the most common fish found in the bay. It is only 7 to 9 inches (18 to 23 cm) long. It is a food source for other bay animals. Pelicans, sharks, and other larger fish eat anchovies. The salmon that live in the bay are important for people living in the area. Fishing for salmon is only allowed during part of the year. This keeps the population of fish strong and healthy.

* When salmon swim against the current, they often leap out of the water.

* Anchovies swim together in large groups called "schools."

Pacific harbor seals are a familiar sight around San Francisco Bay. The seals can be found year-round in the salty waters of the bay. They are large animals, usually weighing close to 300 pounds (136 kilograms). Human activity in the bay has affected the environment of the seals in the past. Today the seal is federally protected from **disturbance**. This means they can't be harassed or hunted by people.

* Harbor seals can live up to 30 years.

Plants live both above and below the water of San Francisco Bay. The underwater plants are known as sea grass. Some include sago pondweed and eelgrass. Sago pondweed can be found in shallow open water. Eelgrass is important for the health of the bay. Eelgrass provides shelter and food for oysters. In response to a loss of eelgrass, the local government has begun a **restoration** project to keep eelgrass growing in the bay.

* Underwater eelgrass still needs the sun in order to grow. It relies on light to come down from the surface.

Fly Away Home

The Pacific Flyway is a migration route that is followed by up to one billion migratory birds each year. It extends from Alaska to South America. San Francisco Bay is an important location on the route. It provides an area for birds to rest, eat, and prepare to continue their journeys.

Areas called riparian forests are home to many of the bay's animals and plants. Riparian forests mark the border between a river and the land. Trees, such as the California bay laurel or cottonwood, grow at the edge of the water. These are tall trees. They grow along with other water plants. In addition to mammals and birds, many amphibians live in these areas. The Pacific tree frog and slender salamander are two common examples.

The wide diversity of environments in the San Francisco Bay watershed provide homes to many types of animals. From fish to birds to mammals, all kinds of wildlife depend on the bay.

CHAPTER 4

Impact on Plants and Animals

The watershed of San Francisco Bay is large. It contains many **tributaries**. Some areas are made up mostly of freshwater. Other areas contain only saltwater. However, different kinds of environments are formed when the two meet. Some of these mixed areas are also affected by the tides of the ocean. The tide brings water back and forth from the ocean.

Tributaries can spread invasive species when they connect with larger bodies of water.

People can stop invasive species, such as the Chinese mitten crab, from spreading by checking their boats when they enter a new body of water.

A tidal flat is an area that changes throughout the day, depending on the tide. When there is a high tide, the tidal flat is full of fish searching for food. During low tide, birds fill the area to eat any fish that remain behind. The plants in a tidal flat include algae and eelgrass. These plants can survive both in and out of the water.

Invasive species are plants or animals that are not **native** to a specific area. When an invasive species enters an area, it can threaten the health of native plants and animals. The Chinese mitten crab is native to China and Korea. It came to San Francisco in 1991 on shrimp boats. These crabs spread up from the mouth of the bay and into the rivers. They dig into sand and make riverbanks unstable.

Water hyacinth arrived in San Francisco Bay from South America in the early 1900s. It was sold to people as a beautiful plant. Water hyacinth is a free-floating plant with big leaves and flowers. People often put it in their gardens. But it does not belong in the bay's waters. It can grow thick, blocking waterways and native plants. It costs the state of California $500,000 every year just to manage and remove water hyacinth from San Francisco Bay and the watershed.

It's not always easy to know if a plant is native or not just by looking at it. Scientists know because they study areas closely.

Fighting back against invasive species is important for the health of the bay. It is also difficult. The first invasive species probably reached the bay 150 years ago. Since 1970 a new invasive species has been discovered every 14 weeks. These often come from ships entering the bay, but they have also come from home aquariums that local residents dump into the water. Even goldfish can be found in low-**elevation** rivers or lakes.

* Although goldfish make good household pets, they are considered an invasive species in lakes and rivers. Goldfish can grow to be very large, and they deplete food sources for native fish.

* Crabs are a common invasive species because they are small and can hold on to moving boats.

CHAPTER 5

Humans and the Bay

San Francisco Bay is a busy place. Millions of people live near the watershed. It is also a popular place for tourists to visit and ships to pass through. Over time, humans have impacted the way the bay is shaped and the animals and plants that live in the bay. People have also worked to improve the bay.

The city of San Francisco is home to over 800,000 residents.

* The Ohlone people lived near San Francisco Bay before European immigrants arrived.

The first humans to live near San Francisco Bay were Native American tribes. They relied on the bay for food. They fished in the water. They also gathered food from the plants that grew there. The first European settlers to reach the area were from Spain. They arrived around 1769.

Since then there have always been towns and cities next to the bay. People built dams along the Sacramento and San Joaquin Rivers. This changed the course of the rivers. As a result, the overall shape and **sediment** in the bay changed. People also dragged boat channels in the rivers and bay. Boat channels make water deeper to allow for larger ships to pass through.

People also began to fill in wetland areas around the bay. Rock and dirt were dumped in order to build up more solid land. Often this rock and dirt came from mines. This brought chemicals into the watershed, including **mercury**. New marshes were created as water moved in different directions.

* Sailors follow shipping lanes through San Francisco Bay to avoid running into shore.

The rich diversity of life in the bay is sometimes threatened by human activity. Human-made pollution has some of the longest-lasting impacts on the bay. Shipping causes a lot of pollution for the bay. Ships can bring oil, gas, and other chemicals into the water. In 1971 two oil tankers crashed, causing more than 800,000 gallons (3,028 cubic meters) of oil to spill into the bay. This was one of the biggest spills in or near the bay. It brought attention to San Francisco Bay. Thousands of volunteers helped clean beaches and marshes. It also made people realize the importance of protecting the bay.

Ships use San Francisco Bay to access ports along the coast of California.

Today many people are working to make sure the plants, animals, and waters of San Francisco Bay are clean and healthy. Organizations like the San Francisco Bay Restoration Authority help save the bay. They fund projects to help wildlife and habitats stay healthy. The United States Environmental Protection Agency (EPA) also plays a role in protecting the bay. It has worked to clean up the mercury present in the bay. The EPA also monitors activity and water quality to make sure federal standards are met.

The EPA is responsible for taking care of all parts of the environment, including water, land, and air.

What Can YOU Do for the Bay?

One of the biggest threats to San Francisco Bay is trash and pollution from nearby cities. Garbage on city streets ends up in storm drains and eventually flows into the bay's waters. Trash in streams and in surrounding wetlands also pollutes the bay.

Organizations like Baykeeper and Save The Bay are working hard to make sure the bay is as clean as possible. People can help these and other organizations by participating in trash cleanup days. Picking up trash in your own neighborhood can help too. And avoiding single-use plastic items like straws and plastic water bottles is a step toward keeping the water of San Francisco Bay clean for future generations.

Human activity has helped make San Francisco Bay famous. The Golden Gate Bridge is one of the most famous **landmarks** in the United States. It is said to be one of the most photographed bridges in the world. It connects San Francisco with Marin County across the bay. Construction on the bridge began in 1933. When the bridge opened in 1937, it was both the longest and tallest suspension bridge in the world. The famous Alcatraz prison is in the middle of the bay. It sits on Alcatraz Island. Nearly 2 million people take a ferry to visit the island each year.

Draw San Francisco Bay

Materials:

* Construction paper in multiple colors (blue, green, brown, etc.)
* Scissors
* Glue or tape
* One large piece of poster board
* Markers, crayons, or colored pencils

Instructions:

1 Break into five groups. Each group should have the same number of students.

2 Your teacher will assign you one chapter (from 1 to 5) from San Francisco Bay.

3 In your group, reread your chapter. As you read, think of all the things your chapter includes that could be part of the picture of San Francisco Bay. Examples: rivers, animals, or people.

4 In your group, draw pictures on the construction paper of everything you can see in your chapter. Use your scissors to cut them out.

5 When every group is finished, your teacher will help you put all of your pictures together on your poster board. Now you have worked together to create San Francisco Bay!

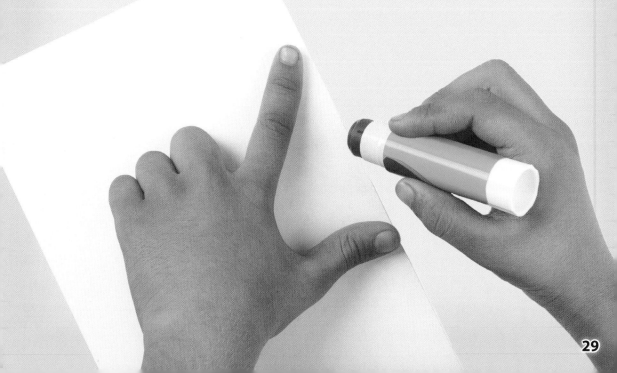

Glossary

abundance *(uh-BUN-dins)* a large amount or number

atmosphere *(AT-muhs-feer)* part of the planet made of air

biosphere *(BYE-oh-sfeer)* part of the planet made of living things

brackish *(BRAK-ish)* water made up of saltwater and river water

delta *(DELTUH)* an area of mud and sand at the mouth of a river

disturbance *(dis-TURB-ence)* an interruption or change in the natural order of an area

elevation *(el-uh-VAY-shin)* the height of something, such as land

estuary *(EHS-choo-air-ee)* area where a river or tributary meets the ocean

forages *(FOR-ihj-iz)* looks for food

geosphere *(JEE-oh-sfeer)* part of the planet made of solid ground

habitats *(HAB-ih-tats)* natural environments where plants and animals live

hydrosphere *(HYE-droh-sfeer)* part of the planet made of water

invasive species *(in-VAY-siv SPEE-sheez)* plants or animals that are not native to an area and cause harm to other species in that area

landmarks *(LAND-marks)* buildings, mountains, and other noticeable features that help people find their way around an area

mercury *(MUR-kyur-ee)* a poisonous element that can be harmful to living things

native *(NAY-tiv)* plant or animal that naturally lives in a location or type of habitat

pollution *(puh-LOO-shin)* when the air, land, or water is dirtied by chemicals, waste, or other harmful things

restoration *(ress-toh-RAY-shin)* returning something to its original state

sediment *(SED-ih-ment)* stones or sand carried in water

tectonic plates *(tek-TAH-nik PLAYTS)* pieces of the Earth's crust that can move

tides *(TYEDZ)* the rhythmic rise and fall of the ocean

tributaries *(TRIH-byu-tair-eez)* smaller rivers or streams that flow into larger rivers or lakes

vital *(VYE-tul)* something that is very important

wetland *(WET-land)* land that is saturated with water, such as marshes and swamps

For More Information

Books

Eggers, Dave. *This Bridge Will Not Be Gray.* San Francisco, CA: Chronicle Books, 2018.

Lawrence, Ellen. *Harbor Seals.* New York, NY: Bearport, 2018.

Medina, Nico, and David Groff. *Where Is Alcatraz?* New York, NY: Penguin Random House, 2016.

Websites

Kids for the Bay
https://kidsforthebay.org
Learn more about how kids just like you work to save the bay!

National Geographic Kids
https://www.natgeokids.com/nz/discover/animals/sea-life/10-blue-whale-facts
You can read more about the whales that are sometimes seen in San Franisco Bay.

San Francisco Facts for Kids
https://kids.kiddle.co/San_Francisco
Find out more about the cities, people, and life in San Francisco.

Index

Alcatraz, 27

crabs, 19

eelgrass, 16, 19

Golden Gate Bridge, 4, 5, 27

harbor seals, 15
Hayward fault, 7
humans, 22, 23, 25

Klamath Mountains, 8

Oakland, California, 5
Ohlone, 23

Pacific Ocean, 5, 8, 10

Ridgway's rail, 13

Sacramento River, 8
salmon, 14
San Andreas fault, 7
San Francisco, California, 3, 4, 5, 7, 8,
    10, 11, 12, 13, 14, 15, 16, 17, 18, 19, 20,
    22, 23, 24, 25, 26, 27
San Joaquin River, 8, 9
San Jose, California, 5
Sierra Nevada Mountains, 8

water hyacinth, 20
watershed, 7, 8, 9, 12, 17, 18, 20, 22, 24

About the Author

M. Weber loves to write for kids. She has written about cities, animals, and the world around us. She lives in Minnesota with her husband and son.